Achieving Success

5 Steps to a Meaningful Career and Rewarding Life

"The Path to Self-Mastery Series"
By Nuakai Aru

TABLE OF CONTENTS

"Think of yourself as dead. You have lived your life.
Now, take what's left and live it properly."
Roman Emperor Marcus Aurelius

ACKNOWLEDGEMENTS

A life that starts and ends with gratitude,
is a joyful path rich in purpose and fulfilment.
Nuakai Aru

This book is lovingly dedicated to my children, Zaia and Lana, and to my nieces and nephews: Roxanne, Shaquari, Andre, Treyvon, Kayah, and Julian. It is my hope that each of you will discover your true path, heed your unique calling, and lead lives enriched with incredible experiences, wonder, meaning and purpose. I extend my deepest gratitude to my ancestors and the Most High for their unwavering support throughout my life journey.

INTRODUCTION

*"The happiness of your life depends upon
the quality of your thoughts."*
Marcus Aurelius

Every person, whether consciously or subconsciously, sets out to discover the meaning and purpose of their life. The age range of 16 to 25 is often seen as a crucial period, where one forms aspirations, explores passions, and establishes plans for the future. However, many individuals end up pursuing careers that only meet their financial needs, losing touch with their true passions and purpose. No matter your age, this eBook can help you discover your authentic purpose through a 7-step roadmap of self-discovery, introspection, and personal insights. Each chapter is laced with timeless wisdom from the writings of the Roman Emperor Marcus Aurelius, as well as modern-day practical tips to help you unlock your inner gifts and create a focused plan for success.

This journey towards self-discovery is no less than a daring adventure, where the traveller is both the explorer and the mapmaker, venturing through the terrain of their inner world. It's an introspective pilgrimage where every step forward is a step into the unknown, a gentle unfolding of the self, often met with a combination of wonder, and at times, apprehension. Your path of Self-Discovery reveals the essence of who you are, what you desire, and ultimately, what gives your existence its intrinsic meaning and purpose.

In a world that constantly nudges us toward predefined norms and prescribed aspirations, embarking on a personal journey to discover one's authentic self becomes a courageous act of rebellion. It's an exploration where you find the purpose that doesn't just echo societal expectations but rings true to your own being. This, therefore, is not a guidebook with predetermined pathways but rather an invitation to weave your tapestry of understanding, to embrace the curious wanderer within, and to find the unique imprints that your soul wishes to leave upon the world.

As you walk carefully on this path, I hope you find the inner strength to acknowledge and respect your vulnerabilities, the courage to embrace your true self, and the wisdom to understand that your journey not only leads to your liberation but also inspires others to start their own journey.

The quote from Roman Emperor Marcus Aurelius at the start of this introduction, "The happiness of your life depends upon the quality of your thoughts," serves as a guiding principle for your life journey. It highlights the profound impact that our internal beliefs, values, and perceptions have on our overall happiness and satisfaction in life. This eBook aims to guide readers, irrespective of age, through a transformative 7-step process of self-discovery. By likening this process to a daring adventure, the chapter emphasizes the significance of introspection, urging readers to look beyond societal expectations and discover their authentic selves. The journey is personal, undefined by external standards, and seeks to uncover one's innate desires and the unique mark one wishes to leave on the world. As you embark on this path, you are encouraged to embrace vulnerability, stay resilient, and remain open to the countless revelations your journey will offer, not only benefiting yourself but also serving as an inspiration for others.

So stride forward, wearing the armour of resilience, but walk gently with an open heart - unrestricted and eager to embrace the wonderful insights your journey will undoubtedly reveal.

STEP 1: INTROSPECTION: THE FOUNDATION OF AWARENESS

"Everything we hear is an opinion, not a fact. Everything we see is a perspective, not the truth."
Marcus Aurelius

Delving into the depths of our minds is like navigating the vast ocean, where emotions are waves, and our deepest desires and fears are hidden treasures. Imagine embarking on an adventure where the terrain explored is not a physical landscape but the vast, intricate world of your own being. This is introspection – a journey inward. It is diving deep into the ocean of your thoughts, riding the waves of your emotions, and unearthing the treasures of your desires and fears.

Introspection is about asking questions without immediate answers, like "What truly makes me happy?" or "Why do I react this way?". It involves pausing, reflecting, and acknowledging your feelings, motivations, and beliefs to understand your true self better. Picture a mental mirror, where you observe not just a reflection, but a doorway into your soul, revealing truths about yourself that were previously hidden or unacknowledged.

This journey might be complex and layered, yet it's profoundly enlightening. By engaging in introspection, you're not only unmasking your authentic self but also laying the foundation upon which your dreams and aspirations are built to create your future. So, take a moment, breathe, and dive within - your internal expedition awaits!

Introspection Exercise:

Grab a Journal: You'll be writing up some personal observations, so have a journal or notebook ready.

Note Your Emotions: As you read through this eBook or generally go about your day, write down moments when you feel:
Happy, Sad, Excited or Bored.

Reflect on Joy: Think deeply about what truly brings happiness and joy to your life. Write down those moments or activities.

Observe Your Natural Interests: Notice which activities totally captivate your attention. Things which seem to make time move much faster or disappear? List these activities.

Discover Your Passion: These observations can provide clues to your deepest passions and joys. They can help highlight what you're naturally inclined to enjoy and excel at.

Continue to use your journal as you go through the eBook as a tool to understand yourself better and guide your future choices. Enjoy the journey of self-discovery!

Questions to Empower
Your Introspection:

What are three moments in your life when you felt the most energized and fulfilled, and why?

Can you describe the situations where you feel most genuine and satisfied? What is behind these feelings?

In terms of helping others, what natural talents do you easily express and why?

Final Thoughts of Step 1:

As you dive deep into the journey of introspection, think of it as navigating the vast oceans of your very essence. This exploration becomes a heartfelt conversation with your core self, unveiling routes to a genuine life. Aurelius' insights act as a beacon during this voyage, reminding you that not everything you hear or see from the outside world is the absolute truth.

Spend time understanding what truly resonates with you – your likes, dislikes, and how you genuinely wish to invest your time. Even if you're just starting and your list seems short, trust that this journey through the book will enrich your understanding. If you've made good progress, commend yourself, but remain open to newer insights and learnings.

Amidst all the external voices and opinions, it's crucial to recognize what's merely someone's perspective and what aligns with your inner truth. When faced with doubts or when negative thoughts emerge, question them. Is it a fact or just an opinion? This distinction helps you weave a life story that genuinely reflects your essence and dreams.

Don't let society's judgments or set standards confine you. Embrace the idea that finding purpose is a personal quest, and success is how you define it. As you forge ahead, shaping your life, let it be a true representation of your unique understanding of purpose, success, and joy.

Remember, as you progress in this introspective journey, Marcus Aurelius' wisdom serves as a guiding light. It encourages you to trust your inner voice and craft a life in tune with your genuine self, leading to real happiness and contentment.

STEP 2: EXPLORATION: BROADENING YOUR HORIZONS

"Waste no more time arguing about what a good man should be. Be one."
Marcus Aurelius

P icture this: you stand at the edge of a vast, alluring wilderness, before you is a world of opportunities, mysteries, and adventures awaiting to be discovered. Exploration is the bold step into the unknown, where every path tread, every corner turned, can unfold new chapters of learning and self-discovery.

Venturing into the unknown is a courageous journey, with each step and turn revealing lessons and insights about oneself. When we talk about "Exploration" in the context of broadening your horizons, we're inviting you to indulge in curiosity and venture into varied experiences, unchained from the familiar. This could be immersing yourself in a new culture, learning a new skill, or simply indulging in a hobby that has always caught your interest, but you've never tried.

It's about breaking free from the cocoon of your comfort zone, challenging your norms, and daring to experience the fullness that life has to offer. Each new endeavour provides an opportunity for newfound knowledge, skills, and passions, gradually revealing a masterpiece of your multifaceted self.

Step forth, let the winds of exploration fill your sails, and steer your consciousness towards unexplored territories. Let your horizon be as broad as there are stars in the night sky; embark on this journey and discover a world of endless possibilities!

Exploration Exercise:

Pick Three New Hobbies or Activities: Choose activities that you've never tried before - it might be painting, martial arts, sports, hiking, a type of dance, learning a new language or gaining a new set of skills.

Commit to At Least Three Sessions: Sign up for a minimum of three classes or sessions per new activity. Push through any discomfort to genuinely give something new a try.

Step Outside Your Comfort Zone: Encourage yourself to embrace new challenges and adventures. Being out of your comfort zone is where you'll grow and gain new insights.

Meet New People and Visit New Places: Explore new places both near and far to learn about different cultures and meet new people.

Maintain an Open Mind: Be receptive to learning and experiencing new things without judgment.

Reflect on Resonance: Pay attention to how these activities resonate with you on a deeper level. Do they align with your inner self?

Record Your Feelings: Write down how each new experience and activity makes you feel and any reflections or thoughts they provoke. In your journal tick off each time you've achieved a part of each exercise.

Most importantly enjoy exploring and learning from each new experience!

Questions for your Exploration:

Is there any skill or experience that you have always been interested in but haven't had the chance to try it out yet?

If failure wasn't a possibility, what's the most daring thing you'd attempt?

If you had unlimited cash flow, how would you spend your time each day? And why?

Final Thoughts of Step 2:

As you stand before the abyss of boundless possibilities, remember that exploration isn't just about seeking —it's about wholeheartedly embracing the wealth of opportunities that come your way. Venture beyond your comfort zone, embrace new experiences and gain deeper insights about both yourself and the world. Every step, every choice, should be infused with purpose, guiding you towards an expansive future. Each new skill and experience you gain adds a unique stitch to the rich tapestry of your life, creating a story filled with dynamic adventures and invaluable lessons.

Yet, in this journey, it's crucial to recall that actions resonate more powerfully than mere words. Discussions about ideals and goodness have their place, but the true essence of growth and influence lives in embodying these ideals. Each day grants us a chance to not just speak of change or goodness but to actively be it. Embrace these moments; let your actions, rather than just your words, sculpt your character and leave an indelible mark on the world.

STEP 3: SELF-KNOWLEDGE: HARNESSING YOUR ASSETS

"When you arise in the morning, think of what a precious privilege it is to be alive, to breathe, to think, to enjoy, to love."
Marcus Aurelius

I magine constructing a majestic castle, symbolising your life's endeavours, where each brick laid is fortified by your skills, strengths, and even your weaknesses. Knowing your skills, strengths and weaknesses is akin to understanding the sturdiest materials and strategic points to build upon, while understanding all vulnerable points to ensure your castle can withstand the tests of time and challenges.

Understanding your abilities is like studying the foundation of a fortress, ensuring its strengths are maximized and vulnerabilities fortified against time's trials. Your skills are your tools, from communication to creativity, that enable you to craft and navigate through life's various scenarios. Strengths, on the other hand, are the natural abilities that give you an edge—your charisma, speed, attention to detail, empathy, analytical prowess, or perhaps, an unyielding resilience.

But let's not forget the role of weaknesses, which are just as pivotal in shaping your unique structure. Everyone has things they struggle with, and they may try to avoid them. These struggles could be related to maths, spelling, punctuality, coordination, or physical strength. However, with attention and effort, these struggles can become a valuable lesson in self-awareness. Recognizing these areas of difficulty doesn't mean that you are weak; it simply highlights where you need to focus your efforts to improve. This recognition presents an opportunity for growth, learning, and development. Embracing your weaknesses allows you to develop really effective coping mechanisms or it can empower you to transform potential vulnerabilities into new strengths, like sturdy, impenetrable walls.

Building is a magical process that goes beyond just constructing something physical. As a builder, you are also a curious learner who gets to discover the secrets embedded in every brick. With each skill, strength, and weakness, you unveil the profound mystery of who you truly are. It's important to harness these assets wisely and create something uniquely magnificent, like a castle that stands tall amidst the landscapes of life's possibilities.

Personal Qualities
Matrix Exercise:

The Qualities Matrix is a powerful tool that lets you gaze into your capabilities, providing a clear picture of your current skill set while also highlighting areas that might need extra improvement or support. By identifying and rating your skills, strengths, and weaknesses, you establish a solid foundation upon which you can build your personal and professional growth.

Here's a step-by-step guide to creating your Skills Matrix:

1. Skills Identification and Rating

Column A: Skills Inventory: Write down a list of all the skills you believe you possess and those you aspire to acquire. This could include technical skills like coding, art, and engineering, or skills like communication, martial arts, maths or specific talents related to your hobbies.

Column B: Proficiency Rating: Assign a rating from 1 (novice) to 10 (expert) based on your current proficiency in each skill.

2. Strengths Identification and Rating

Column A: Strengths Inventory: List down all your strengths. Strengths are inherent traits or abilities, such as being smart, empathetic, loyal, hardworking, detail-oriented, compassionate, loving, articulate, strong, accurate, fast or resilient.

Column B: Confidence Rating: Rate each strength based on how confidently you can utilize it in various situations, using a scale of 1 (low confidence) to 10 (high confidence).

3. Weaknesses Identification and Rating

Column A: Weaknesses Inventory: Identify areas you find challenging or aspects of your personality that might need refinement, such as impatient, easily distracted, quick to anger, overly shy, uncoordinated, forgetful, passive, lazy, indecisive, physically weak or stiff.

Column B: Improvement Urgency: Rate each weakness on a scale of 1 (less urgent) to 10 (very urgent) based on how urgently you feel the need to work on it.

Organizing your skills and qualities in a structured manner through the Qualities Matrix can provide you with a clear view of where you currently stand and inspire you to move closer to the skills and qualities you aspire to have. This matrix acts like a mirror - reflecting your present self - and a window - revealing your desired self - enabling you to bridge the gap between the two with clarity and vision. By identifying your inherent skills, natural strengths, areas for improvement, and differentiating between what you're good at and what you love, the matrix becomes a map guiding you in your personal development journey. This map helps you recognize how your unique attributes can contribute to the world.

Questions to Increase Your Knowledge of Self

When have you felt most proud of an accomplishment? What skills or strengths did you use to achieve it?

In what situations have you felt overwhelmed or out of your depth? What was the primary challenge?

If you were to teach someone, what skill or subject would you feel confident in sharing? Conversely, which topics would you prefer to avoid?

Final Thoughts of Step 3:

Each day, as we arise, is a testament to the miracle of existence. Embracing the joys of life and connecting deeply with ourselves and others is not just a celebration of being alive but also an acknowledgement of the grand castle of our potential. This castle is constructed upon the inherent abilities, strengths, and weaknesses that craft our unique identity.

Marcus Aurelius reminds us that each day is truly a gift, and an opportunity— from the standard acts of breathing, and thinking, to the profound acts of feeling and loving. These are not just merely acts but rather key points of gratitude that anchor and drive us forward on our journey of self-discovery and growth.

As we delve into this introspective journey, it becomes crucial to consistently review our qualities matrix. This daily practice enables us to capitalize on our strengths and actively develop the areas that need more nurture. This introspection and self-awareness ensure that we remain grounded yet open to growth, making us unshakeable amidst life's challenges.

As you continue to explore your life's adventures, always remember to appreciate the essence of each day and the opportunities it brings, strengthening your foundation and enriching your every moment.

STEP 4:
TRANSFORMATION:
DREAMS INTO REALITY

"If it is not right, do not do it; if it is not true, do not say it."
Marcus Aurelius

See your dreams as seeds, plant them, feed them and prepare for them to bloom. Dive into your career path where passions and skills unite to create a rewarding profession. Exploring practical job opportunities involves transforming your aspirations and imaginative notions into a feasible career path. It entails exploring various avenues in which your talents, passions, and interests can lead to a flourishing and satisfying professional journey. Think chefs turning culinary passions into gourmet creations, or tech-savvy innovators advancing into the thrilling domains of AI and virtual reality! Your enchanting dream world brims with potential – let's explore, adapt, and strategically navigate towards making those dreams a thrilling reality!

There are many fulfilling jobs that can lead to a meaningful life. Here are some options to consider.

1. Creative Careers: Unleash Your Artistic Spirit

Delve into various creative domains including arts, music, writing, and design to unearth where your inventive inclinations bloom. Engage in artistic workshops, collaborate with veteran creators, and present your creations to find your ideal creative niche.

Example Job Roles:

Graphic Designer
Content Writer
Music Producer

Fashion Designer
Photographer / Film-maker

2. Logical Endeavours: Navigate the World of Reason

Plunge into the realms of research, coding, problem-solving, and analytics, exploring varied facets such as computer science, mathematics, and scientific research. Participate in analytical projects, solve real-world problems, join relevant communities, and network with professionals to determine where your logical aptitudes can truly shine.

Example Job Roles:

Data Analyst
Software Engineer
Research Scientist
Mathematician
Information Security Analyst

3. Practical Work: Building Visible, Impactful Results

Engage in sectors where your endeavours materialize into tangible outputs such as carpentry, personal training, coaching, and event management. Participate in hands-on workshops, work alongside skilled professionals, complete real-world projects, and see your efforts physically take shape, uncovering where your pragmatic talents are most effectively utilized.

Example Job Roles:

Event Coordinator
Personal Trainer
Carpenter
Physiotherapist

Agricultural Manager

4. Passion Projects: Turning Enthusiasm into Achievement

It's always a good idea to channel your hobbies and interests into ventures that can have a positive impact on others and potentially generate income. Whether you enjoy painting, cooking, teaching, adventuring, entertaining or creative endeavours, you should consider ways to monetize your skills to create social impact. Attend workshops and events to expand your network with like-minded people and learn about market dynamics that can help you turn your passions into a successful and fulfilling business.

Example Job Roles - Dependent on Your Passion

Personal Chef (Cooking)
Fitness Blogger (Fitness and Writing)
Custom Furniture Maker (Carpentry or Woodworking)
Online Art Teacher (Art and Teaching)
Indie Game Developer (Gaming and Coding)
Embark on each journey with an eager mind and an open heart, allowing your experiences to guide you towards a career where your passions and skills intertwine harmoniously. Sometimes gaining industry experience is the best way to develop skills before starting your own business. Embrace each path enthusiastically and learn from all the experiences they offer.

Dreams into Reality Exercise Quiz:

This questionnaire quiz will shed light on the career paths that can be harmonious with your higher meaning and purpose. Answer each question truthfully and intuitively to get the most accurate guidance.

1.   Identifying Core Values
Select the top 3 values that resonate most with you.

A. Creativity
B. Community
C. Justice
D. Innovation
E. Sustainability
F. Empathy
G. Integrity
H. Leadership

2.   Interacting with Others
Which statement best describes your interaction with others?

A. I love to lead and inspire a team.
B. I prefer one-on-one deep connections.
C. I enjoy collaborating and co-creating.
D. I work best independently, with autonomy.

3.   Embracing Challenges
How do you approach problems or challenges?

A. I seek innovative and ground-breaking solutions.
B. I lean on tried-and-true methods.
C. I collaborate with others for collective solutions.
D. I seek wisdom and perspective from past experiences.

4.   Daily Tasks and Responsibilities
How would you prefer to spend your working hours?

A. Engaging with people and building relationships.
B. Analysing data and finding patterns.
C. Creating, designing, or inventing things.
D. Planning, organizing, and executing projects.

5.   Impacting the World
Which statement best describes your desired impact on the world?

A. I want to drive technological or scientific advancements.
B. I want to advocate for social justice and equity.
C. I want to contribute to environmental sustainability.
D. I want to inspire and empower others through arts or media.

6.   Workplace Environment
What type of workplace environment resonates with you the most?

A. Structured and traditional
B. Dynamic and ever-changing
C. Supportive and team-oriented
D. Independent and flexible

7.   Championing a Cause
If you could champion one cause through your work, what would it be?

A. Global health and well-being
B. Equality and social justice
C. Climate change and sustainability
D. Education and empowerment

Results:
Based on your responses, if you have predominantly selected one of the letters A, B, C, or D, the following career options may be a good fit for you. However, if your answers are a mix of these options, you may find fulfilment and purpose in pursuing a few of the options listed below.

Majority A's:
You might find fulfilment in Innovative and Leadership Roles, possibly within technology, science, or start-up environments, driving change and advancements.

Majority B's:
A career in Social Advocacy or Counselling may align with your values. You could work towards societal well-being and justice, ensuring that voices are heard and respected.

Majority C's:
Consider exploring careers in Environmental Sustainability and Collaboration. You might thrive in roles that allow you to protect our planet and work collectively toward a greener future.

Majority D's:
A path in Creative and Empowering Fields, such as the arts, media, or education, might bring you closer to your higher purpose, allowing you to inspire and uplift others.

Understanding the blend of letters (A, B, C, D)
Having multiple letters in your answers can reveal a vast array of preferences, strengths, and interests. A diverse mix in your responses indicates multifaceted interests and potential careers that intersect various areas.

It is important to remember that these results offer a

flexible framework, not a strict directive. They serve as a starting point to identify potential paths but should be accompanied by additional self-exploration, taking into account your intrinsic values, specific skill sets, and career aspirations

Dreams into Reality Questions

Unearth Your Passions:

If you could solve one global issue, what would it be and how could you contribute to its resolution?

Visualise Your Future Self:

Imagine reflecting on your career at retirement. What achievements or contributions would make you feel the proudest? What does success truly mean to you, and what steps can you take now to start that journey?

Aligning Values with Profession:

Can you think of a time when you felt completely fulfilled and purposeful? What were you doing at that moment and why did it feel so rewarding? How can you incorporate the key elements of that experience into your career to ensure that it consistently provides you with a sense of purpose and aligns with your values?

Final Thoughts of Step 4:

Living in alignment with our core truths and values is the bedrock of a purposeful life and career. To navigate the path from dreams to reality effectively, it's pivotal to recognize these foundational values and let them direct your career choices. Align your passions with practical routes, and always be open to change and lifelong learning. By doing so, you not only harness the full potential of every opportunity but also utilize your skills to leave a positive mark on the world.

Furthermore, this journey is enriched by the company you keep. Surrounding yourself with mentors and peers who share your values can amplify your progress. They provide invaluable insights, fresh perspectives, and the heartfelt companionship needed to ensure each step you take is enriched with integrity, authenticity, and purpose. Through this harmonious blend of self-awareness and supportive networking, you are set to transform your dreams into reality with clarity and conviction.

STEP 5: VISION BUILDING: BLUEPRINT FOR YOUR FUTURE

"Very little is needed to make a happy life; it is all within yourself, in your way of thinking."
Marcus Aurelius

E nvision this: a ship, fully stocked and gleaming with provisions, eagerly sways at the harbour, ready to traverse the boundless ocean ahead. This is your vessel, primed to sail into the expansive seas of the future. But wait, where is it headed? Vision Building is the art of crafting a vibrant, detailed, and alluring map, that can guide you towards the abundant destination of your dreams. It's more than a direction; it's a promise, a commitment to steer your vessel with purpose and passion across the infinite possibilities of tomorrow.

A vision doesn't demand perfection; it seeks authenticity. It's a reflection of your deepest aspirations, a lighthouse illuminating the path even when the seas are stormy. It is your unwavering North Star in the vast, uncharted waters of life's possibilities.

"So, hoist your sails, or start your engine and with a compass crafted from your very dreams, let the winds of your life vision build a direct course to lead your journey to the distant locations known only by your heart."

Vision Building Exercise: My Pathway to a Successful Future

The purpose of this exercise is to help you create a detailed and tailored plan for achieving success in both your personal and professional life. By combining your career goals, personal growth, and work-life balance, you can build a clear and attainable roadmap towards success. The plan should be easy to understand and visually appealing, guiding you towards your desired outcomes.

1.   Draw Your Timeline of Success:
Represent your future in a visually compelling timeline, spanning from now until your targeted milestone (e.g., 1, 2, 5, 10, or 20 years into the future). This should be a combination of personal and professional goals, which include financial goals, family intentions, educational aims, and personal objectives and dreams.

2.   Identify Your Key Milestones:
Pin down significant milestones along your timeline. These could include educational and career achievements, personal development goals and milestones of achievement or key life events. Be sure to allocate a tentative date for each milestone.

3.   Develop Mini-Goals:
Under each milestone, list smaller goals or steps that will guide you toward achieving your larger goals. Include both professional and personal goals to ensure a balanced approach to the blueprint of your future.

4.   SMART Check:

Review each milestone goal, refining them according to the SMART criteria. (Specific, Measurable, Achievable, Relevant, Time-Bound)

SMART GOALS CHECK:

Specific: Clearly state your goal (e.g., Purchase a 3-bedroom house in a [Specific City/Neighbourhood], within a budget of £300,000.

Measurable: Define success (e.g., Save £60,000 for a 20% down payment.) To save £60,000 by saving £1,000 per month, it will take 60 months, or 5 years, to achieve the down payment goal.

Achievable: Ensure that the monthly savings goal is feasible without straining other financial obligations. Evaluate current savings and monthly income. Ensure eligibility for a home loan of $240,000. Validate that the anticipated mortgage payment is manageable.

Relevant: Align it with your broader dreams. Ensure the house size, type, and location align with your lifestyle, commute, and potential future family plans. Ensure that the house and location align with your 5-10-year personal and professional plans.

Time-Bound: Set a deadline (e.g., "by a specific year"). Plan to accumulate the down payment within 5 years, considering the monthly saving goal. Begin house hunting once the down payment is secured. Aim to finalize the purchase within 6 months from the start of the active search.

5. Celebrate Wins:
Decide in advance how you'll celebrate reaching each

milestone. Giving yourself a pat on the back is a crucial way of empowering further sacrifices and achievement!

6.   Check-In Regularly:

Sometimes you may lose sight of or get distracted by your main life goals. Make time to look over your plan and check in every now and then to make sure you're on track.

7.   Flex and Adapt:

It is not the strongest of the species that survives, nor the most intelligent; it is the one most adaptable to change. In the same way, the best planners are those who adapt their plans as they proceed. Keep making time to improve and adapt your goals and milestones as your plan unfolds leading you to success.

This Vision Building exercise will provide you with a written visual and easy-to-follow guide that can keep you focused with clear goals and manageable milestones, ensuring you remain motivated and on track.

Questions to Inspire
Vision Building

What Legacy Do You Want to Leave?
Dive deep and explore what you want to be remembered for. Envision the impacts you wish to make on your community, industry, or the world, and how these align with your personal values and passions.

How can your vision for life include continuous learning and growth?
Exploring how your future self continues to evolve and learn pinpoints a commitment to ongoing development, ensuring your vision remains dynamic and adaptable through time.

What Does Success Look Like to You?
Moving away from generic definitions, visualizing your unique portrayal of success ensures that your vision aligns deeply with your individual desires and values, promoting authentic fulfilment.

Final Thoughts of Step 5:

Moving forward in life requires more than just ambition —it calls for a blend of clear planning, introspection, and unwavering positivity. Start by crafting a well-defined vision for your journey, rooted not only in the tangible goals you aim to achieve but also in the personal growth you wish to experience. Recognise that true happiness isn't just about reaching a destination but is found within the steps you take. With a positive mindset, even the hardest days can reveal moments of joy and profound discovery.

When you draft your roadmap, use SMART criteria to ensure each goal is actionable and achievable. This approach not only gives you a clear direction but also acts as a beacon during times of doubt, ensuring that you remain adaptable and focused on your path to fulfilment.

Yet, beyond any plan or strategy, remember the power of your perspective. Your internal mindset—how you perceive challenges, celebrate successes, continually learn from all experiences, and embrace the unexpected—will be the strongest determining factor of your journey. Amidst the intricacies and unpredictability of life, let this wisdom guide you, remember, "Your external world often mirrors your internal state". By intertwining a well-thought-out vision with a positive way of thinking, you not only pave the way for success but also ensure each step is taken with purpose, gratitude, and fulfilment. Celebrate the milestones you achieve, continually adapt with determination, and draw motivation from both the challenges you overcome and the joys you experience.

CONCLUSION

*"Because your own strength is unequal to the
task, do not assume that it is beyond
the powers of man; but if anything is within
the powers and province of man,
believe that it is within your own compass also."*
Marcus Aurelius

In this quote, Marcus Aurelius reminds us that just because we find a task challenging or feel incapable of accomplishing it, it doesn't mean it's impossible for humans in general. If someone has done it or can do it, then you too possess the potential to achieve it. Embrace the belief that your potential is immense, yet still largely uncharted. Challenges are not signs of your limitations, but invitations to grow, evolve, and uncover strengths previously unknown to you. When you see others achieving their dreams, see it as motivation, for it attests to what's achievable for everyone, including you.

Success unfolds daily through meticulous planning, unwavering dedication, and persistent effort. Unravelling your life's true purpose isn't a one-time revelation but a perpetual journey, adapting as you mature and evolve. It transcends merely settling on a career or a singular passion; it involves understanding your unique place in the world and how you can enhance it. Life's voyage isn't always straightforward. There will be times of reflection, redirection, and rediscovery, and that's okay.

Your journey is distinctively yours. Cherish it, garner wisdom from it, and above all, relish the adventure of self-exploration and purpose cultivation. Remember, the world eagerly anticipates the distinct magic only you can bring forth.

> *"Find your purpose, live with meaning, and*
> *every moment becomes an exciting step*
> *towards your living legacy."*

Nuakai Aru

If you found this book useful and informative, I would love to hear your feedback. Please consider leaving a review to share your thoughts and experiences. Your valuable insights will not only be greatly appreciated, but they will also help other readers on their journey.

Thank you for your kindness and I wish you great success as you continue your journey!

THE ROMAN EMPEROR
MARCUS AURELIUS

"Today I escaped anxiety. Or no, I discarded it, because it was within me, in my own perceptions — not outside."
Marcus Aurelius

orn in 121 ACE, Marcus Aurelius ascended the Roman throne in 161 ACE and ruled until 180 ACE, during a pivotal period in the vast tapestry of Roman history. Set against the backdrop of the Pax Romana, his reign was a time of relative peace and stability throughout the Roman Empire. However, despite the broader peace, his leadership faced challenges such as the Parthian War, the Germanic wars, and the devastating Antonine Plague.

At this time, Rome was the uncontested superpower of the Mediterranean and beyond, with territories stretching from Britain in the West to Mesopotamia in the East. Its intricate road networks, architectural marvels, and formidable legions spoke of its influence and dominance. However, other civilizations, like the Han Dynasty in China, were also flourishing, making notable advancements in various fields. Ancient Egypt, with its millennia of rich history, now played a crucial role as a grain supplier for Rome, and its cultural legacy added depth to Rome's already diverse tapestry.

Within this vast empire, Marcus Aurelius stood out as a beacon of wisdom and introspection. Despite commanding unmatched power, he was deeply committed to Stoic philosophy, a school of thought emphasizing virtue and wisdom over material wealth. This commitment is evident in his personal diary, "Meditations", which offers a glimpse into his reflections on personal integrity, self-control, and resilience, rather than the might of the empire.

It's profound that an emperor, arguably the most influential individual of his time, was so deeply introspective. His Stoic beliefs weren't just personal; they informed his leadership style. Marcus Aurelius viewed his role not as an avenue for personal gain but as a solemn duty to the greater good, his empire and its people. This perspective was instrumental in navigating the myriad challenges during his reign.

In conclusion, Marcus Aurelius's insights into the human psyche, ethics, and leadership provide a rare look into the soul of a ruler who, despite wielding immense power, remained grounded in the pursuit of wisdom and virtue, leaving a legacy that transcends time.

10 QUOTES FROM MARCUS AURELIUS MEDITATIONS

"The happiness of your life depends upon the quality of your thoughts."

"Everything we hear is an opinion, not a fact. Everything we see is a perspective, not the truth."

"Waste no more time arguing about what a good man should be. Be one."

"When you arise in the morning, think of what a precious privilege it is to be alive, to breathe, to think, to enjoy, to love."

"If it is not right, do not do it; if it is not true, do not say it."

"Very little is needed to make a happy life; it is all within yourself, in your way of thinking."

"Because your own strength is unequal to the task, do not assume that it is beyond the powers of man; but if anything is within the powers and province of man, believe that it is within your own compass also."

"Today I escaped anxiety. Or no, I discarded it, because it was within me, in my own perceptions — not outside."

"Think of yourself as dead. You have lived your life.

Now, take what's left and live it properly."

"Everything that happens is either endurable or not.
If it's endurable, then endure it. Stop complaining.
If it's unendurable ... then stop complaining. Your
destruction will mean its end as well."

"The universe is change; our life is what our thoughts make it."

ABOUT THE AUTHOR

Nuakai Aru is a dual-heritage Jamaican-British polymath, with a tapestry of talents ranging from award-winning film directing to teaching celebrities martial arts. As a writer, producer, actor, and wellbeing coach, his multi-dimensional life paints a canvas of rich experiences, fostering a broad perspective. Raised by a British single mother, his mixed heritage spurred him on a profound quest for knowledge of self and our collective story.

His personal investigation led him to travel to over 40 countries around the world, where his personal story became seamlessly woven into the tapestry of human history, culture, and spirituality. From the Pyramids of Giza and the ancient wonders of Angkor Wat to Stonehenge in the UK and the Mayan ruins of Belize, his experiences merged ancient marvels with contemporary reflections of the world. As a modern-day griot, he champions overlooked stories, crafting socially conscious films that merge history, culture, and global narratives. Beyond his professional pursuits, Nuakai's sense of adventure has empowered him to follow his inner calling and live by the wisdom of his passions. He has climbed distant mountain peaks, navigated untouched wildernesses, parachuted from great heights, and taken part in scientific scuba diving adventures. He has also endured prolonged fasts, participated in plant medicine ceremonies, and mastered himself through full-contact martial arts. Through these experiences, Nuakai has come to realise that the most profound adventure one can go on, is the one inward to discover the fullness of self.

With over three decades of experience in martial arts, Nuakai has honed skills across a spectrum of disciplines, from Muay Thai and Western Boxing to weapons training and Qi Gong. Beyond his combative pursuits, he has dedicated over two decades to diverse holistic practices for personal development, including hand acupuncture, massage, reiki, life coaching, and mentoring. Now, for over a decade, he's generously imparted his knowledge, wisdom, and practical insights to others through group settings and private classes.

An example of this is his integrated wellbeing system called "BEING", which exemplifies his commitment to personal and collective growth. Grounded in his holistic BeMS Tetrad philosophy, it's a harmonious fusion of physical, emotional, mental, and spiritual development. His forthcoming book, "The Warrior in the Garden," seamlessly melds his diverse world of experiences, offering readers an intimate guide to self-mastery.

Amidst a global landscape of turbulence and perpetual evolution, Nuakai Aru is dedicated to enhancing both individual and societal well-being. With a diverse array of offerings - including films, art, writings, classes, and events - his aim is to inspire and uplift those around him. Through every endeavour, he strives to guide and support others to reach their full potential.

"THE PATH TO SELF-MASTERY SERIES"

Additional books in the series:

The Warrior in the Garden: A Humble Guide to Self-Mastery
Archetypes of Higher Consciousness: Principles of Mental
Mastery (Coming Soon)

Achieving Success: 5 Steps to a Meaningful Career and
Rewarding Life

Films Directed by the Author:

HumaniTree: A Story of Us Humans Across the Globe
Warrior Spirit: Forged in the Fires of Muay Thai
Africa's Black Star: The Rise and Fall of Kwame Nkrumah
Nubian Spirit: The African Legacy of the Nile Valley
The Lion Mountains: A Journey Through Sierra Leones
History

For more visit: www.The-Cosmic-Path.com

Printed in Great Britain
by Amazon

34804801R00036